Wha.. ..
Bind on Earth

A Historical Record of How God Warned About Hurricane Irene.

Incontrovertible Evidence That God Still Speaks Today.

Randal L. Cutter

Distributed by: New Dawn Ministries
9335 W. Sample Road
Coral Springs, FL 33065
www.newdawn.org

DEDICATION

To the One who initiated this story, Jesus the Christ;

*With appreciation to my incredibly gifted wife, Dawn,
And my wonderful children, Alyssa, Linea, and Joshua;
And to all my prophetic mentors.*

*In Remembrance of Bob Jones, a mentor and friend,
Who, after Irene, would often approach me and ask,
"Have you seen it?" referring to a hurricane or storm that
the Lord has shown to him, and over which Bob would
challenge us to pray.*

CONTENTS

ACKNOWLEDGMENTS

To the Members of
New Dawn Community Church, past and present.
Thank you for pursuing the Lord with me.

PREFACE

On October 1, 1999, WPTV, the NBC affiliate in West Palm Beach, Florida, aired a report on a church in Coral Springs, Florida, which had predicted that a hurricane named Irene would strike southeast Florida by surprise.

That interview, broadcast twelve days before the storm that would become Hurricane Irene had even formed, has become eloquent testimony for the veracity of everything contained in this book.

You can read this book without watching the interview, available at the link below. However, if you watch the video, you will want to continue reading this book.

The video is evidence that God still speaks.

Video Links:

HurricaneIrene.com

YouTube Reference: JVsb6Pk-qm8

INTRODUCTION

Not too long ago, I heard the voice of God in a dream. He said, "I remember Irene. I remember Irene."

I immediately woke up, and wondered at what I had heard. I knew who Irene was, or rather, I knew what Irene was. She was a hurricane that had hit our area of South Florida in 1999. She was also a major part of my history, and the history of my congregation, New Dawn Community Church.

The Lord had told us about Irene a year before she came to our area. He had told us her name, where she was going to hit, and the area in most danger. He also told us that she would confound forecasters and would hit our area by surprise as a category four storm. If you can imagine what Hurricane Katrina of 2005 would have done to the southern gulf coast if she had hit by surprise, then you understand the absolute catastrophe the Lord had described to us. But there was a bright ray of hope. He also invited us to call area Christians together to pray, and showed us that our prayers could reduce the intensity of the storm and release much protection to South Florida.

We accepted his invitation, and called the churches of Broward County, Florida to pray from March to October of 1999. The pastors of Broward County, at least the ones who were here in 1999, remember those events. Even more people remember because a local NBC affiliate heard of our prayer efforts, interviewed me, and broadcast our call to prayer before the storm even formed (you can still see the broadcast at hurricaneirene.com). Much of South Florida's attention was on Irene months before she made her appearance.

Irene hit us on October 15, 1999, as a category one hurricane. Everything the Lord showed us about Irene was exactly accurate. As he had promised, because we had prayed, the storm's intensity had diminished. He gave his Church in Broward County a great victory by protecting us from a category four storm. He also gave his Church a great victory by publicly demonstrating that it was possible to hear from God about something like this, and that it was possible to do something about what God was showing us. We had bound on earth what he had bound in heaven.

Since that day, we have grown in our understanding of intercessory authority, and the role God has given his Church to play. God wants his Church to use the authority he has given it to protect lives, to stop or reduce the intensity of natural disasters, and to release blessing on the earth. These are things that we now readily see, but that we didn't understand when God first issued the invitation.

When the Lord told me that he remembered Irene, I knew that it was time, once again, for me to remember Irene. When the Lord repeats himself, it means that a matter is

3

firmly established; and when he remembers something, he wants to do something about it. This book is part of what the Lord wanted to do.

You are holding an invitation in your hands. The facts of the basic story are not in dispute. Over fifty pastors and churches from across the theological spectrum were called as witnesses to what God was doing in 1999. The Lord even marshaled the resources of an NBC affiliate to document the truth of this book. The Lord took such care to document the facts for your sake. He is inviting you to participate in what will become the greatest age of his Church. He is inviting you to make a difference in this world for the age to come. He is inviting you to remember Irene, and to then enter into your destiny as you remember her.

The Lord remembers Irene. Now you will, too.

1

PREPARING A TEACHER

I remember the first time I heard God's voice. Actually, I should say that I remember the first time that God spoke to me, and I knew it was the Lord who was speaking to me. It wasn't that his voice was audible. In fact, since I was mowing the lawn at the time, if it had been audible, the Lord would have been competing with the roar of the lawn mower. Instead, the voice that I heard spoke clearly, with an unmistakable resonance and meter into my spirit and my conscious thoughts. The racket of the lawn mower faded away as the sound of eternity permeated my soul.

I had oft dreamed about what it might be like to have the Lord speak to me. I would read the prophets or their histories in the Bible, and I would wonder what it must have been like to have the Creator share his thoughts with them. I assumed that this line of thought would always remain a flight of fancy. I was part of a denomination that had taught me that God doesn't speak to us anymore apart from the Bible. I was in agreement with this theological perspective, so I certainly wasn't seeking an encounter with God when he spoke to me. However, I was praying.

Well, I like to call it praying. It was really more like complaining. I was letting the Lord know some of the injustice that was occurring in my life, and I'm absolutely certain that there was more than a touch of self-pity mixed into my murmuring prayer. My finances were difficult, and I was letting God know that he wasn't treating his servant that well.

I had graduated from seminary in May of 1987. The denomination to which I belonged sent me to South Florida to work in a church plant under the auspices of their mission board. I quickly found out that South Florida had a much higher cost of living than Wisconsin, my home state. My salary was such that I would have been very hard pressed to make ends meet in Wisconsin. In Broward County, Florida, it was impossible.

When we first arrived in Florida we didn't realize that we were poor. Dawn, my wife, and I were married in the summer of 1980, and I immediately started a seven year education program in order to become a pastor in our denomination. We were well aware of the fact that we were poor all through college and seminary. We regularly saw the Lord meet our financial needs in amazing, almost miraculous ways throughout the years of education. However, when we came to South Florida, I started to receive a salary as a church planter, and Dawn began to work at a daycare. We felt fabulously rich even though our relatively meager incomes were far less than the average household income in our city.

Our delusion about our financial welfare was shattered when we had our first child in the spring of 1989. Dawn and I had decided that when the Lord granted us children, she would stay home in order to give them the best possible launch into their life purposes. So, while Dawn had not been making a great deal of money at the daycare, it had still helped make ends meet. When she was forced to stop working earlier than we expected because of a high-risk pregnancy, we quickly found out that even without the extra costs of a high-risk pregnancy, those ends didn't meet anymore.

By the fall of 1989, I was stressed about our finances. I did some of my best complaining—I called it praying—while mowing the lawn. I was using an old push mower that had been donated by a gracious family from our congregation when they discovered I could not afford a mower. They were not people of means, so they gave what they had. Unfortunately for me, what they had was an old push mower with wobbly wheels that caused the mower to sink into South Florida's spongy St. Augustine grass. As a result, the lawn mower pushed like a tank. Add Florida's high humidity and high temperatures to this equation, and you can understand why mowing brought out this Wisconsin boy's most eloquent financial prayers.

So there I was, one warm day in 1989, having a one-sided conversation with the Lord about how bad things were, and how I needed some major help if things were going to turn around. I remember right where I was on the yard when the Lord spoke to me. I suspect he decided that this one-sided conversation wasn't going anywhere good, and so he interrupted me. With volume loud enough to silence my prayers and shake my being, he said, "It's your fault."

I suspect that most of us have imagined what it would be like to hear the voice of God. We probably fantasize about the holiness of the moment, or the sacred nature of the conversation. We might indulge in considering how that moment would change us forever, and how everything would be different after this divine encounter. That is not at all how it seemed to me. I was so absolutely indignant about what the Lord said, that I even forgot that I didn't believe this type of thing could happen. I wasn't awed by the encounter; I was aggravated.

I responded to the Lord's charge at once. I wasn't going to simply accept what the voice had said. With more than a hint of anger and exasperation I asked, "What do you mean?" I couldn't imagine how the current state of affairs was my fault. However, his answer cut through my anger, my delusion about my situation, and all of my carefully constructed arguments about why I was the victim in this situation.

His clear, vibrant voice shook my being one more time as he answered, "You are the teacher."

I learned at that moment, and have become more familiar with it since, that when the Lord speaks to you like this, he also opens up the eyes of your understanding so that you hear everything he is communicating. When Jesus appeared to his disciples after his resurrection, we are told that he **"opened their minds" (Luke 24:45 NIV).** I believe that is exactly what happened when the Lord spoke to me. My mind opened and I understood exactly what he meant. I could instantly see things from his perspective, and I did not like what I saw.

I had been trained in a denomination that still believed that God's Word was vital. In order to gain entrance to their seminary, you had to have three years of Greek language education and two years of Hebrew language education. The denomination believed that in order to correctly handle the Word of God, you needed to read and understand the grammar of the original Hebrew and Greek since the Holy

Spirit had chosen to use those languages. They wanted students who were not only comfortable with the Hebrew and Greek languages, but also were capable of having scholarly debate about the nuances of the grammar in each passage of scripture.

I had excelled in these language studies, and prided myself in being able to teach God's truth from the original languages. I had delved deeply into the Word since my graduation, and had grown greatly in my understanding. But there was one area of study I diligently avoided because it held no interest for me. I chose to ignore any study of what the Bible said about the stewardship of finances.

To be absolutely honest, I hated talking about money in church. I didn't want to discuss giving, and I certainly didn't want to discuss my salary. In the two years I had been in South Florida, I had only taught and preached on stewardship topics a couple of times, and understood very little on the topic. I had the tools at hand to do the study, provided by the Lord through the training system I had attended, but I had chosen not to use those tools to study about finances.

When God told me I was the teacher, he was telling me I had a responsibility to dig into the word, understand it, and train my people in the whole counsel of God. If the members of the congregation were not contributing at an appropriate level, or if the salary that they were paying me was inadequate, I could not complain. If I had done my job, if I had sought to thoroughly understand God's Word on those topics, and imparted that truth to my congregation, then maybe I would have had cause to be upset. As it stood, I was a teacher who was not doing what he had been called to do on this particular topic of study. I was guilty as charged; it was my fault.

It didn't take long after that for me to dive into what the Bible said about finances, and honestly, it did not take long for that teaching to change the congregation and my own personal circumstance. I will keep those details for a future book on God's supernatural economy. However, I can mention that the giving patterns in my congregation changed so drastically in such a short period of time, that some officials from the denomination asked me to write a study on stewardship for them. Though I never published the study, the fact that I was asked to write it demonstrates the impact that the brief encounter with the Lord unleashed in my life.

As wonderful as this result was, and as fascinating as Biblical finances can be, the Lord had far more in mind than simply helping me understand about finances on that day in 1989. He was beginning the slow, patient process of shaping my character and my heart so that I could hear him better, and so that he could use me more fully. I didn't fully appreciate it at the time, but the Lord really loves South Florida. He also knew something else that I did not know; a catastrophe was headed toward South Florida, and he was preparing me to help stop it.

2

PREPARING A PEOPLE

I do not understand everything about the Lord's preparation process; his thoughts really are not our thoughts. Most of our lives we are being prepared for his purposes, but to us it feels like normal life. I went about my job of leading my congregation, never guessing that the Lord was preparing us to release his protection over our area. Since this would not be an easy job, the Lord needed to mold my congregation into a team that he could use. That process did not happen quickly, nor was it pain-free.

After my encounter with the Lord, I added several things to my study agenda. First, as the Lord had directed, I began to study what the Bible had to say about finances. And second, and even more important in the long term, I also began to compare my experience with God to what the Bible taught on that topic. I believed then, as I do now, that the Bible is the inspired Word of God. I knew that the Lord would not contradict the Bible by what he did or by what he said. As I studied the Bible, it was easy to see that what the Lord had said to me did not contradict his written Word. However, I had to make certain that the experience itself was consistent with what the Bible said. I had been taught that God no longer spoke to individuals in this fashion. I now needed to determine if the Bible clearly stated that God does not speak to his people as he always had in the past.

My studies lead me to realize that the Bible never says that God will not speak to us as individuals. It clearly teaches that he will never contradict his written word in these communications. And since the Bible is complete, and those who had been called to pen the Holy Writ have long since passed into eternity, these communications would not be new scriptures. They could, however, be words of strength, comfort, encouragement, and personal direction. The Bible is sufficient for our salvation, but his voice is important for personal direction.

I realize that there are many books and theologies that have been written that say that God will not speak to individuals today. I also realize that they do not use clear statements of scripture to make their point. They build a logical argument based upon other biblical truths, or what they believe particular passages mean, and then they deduce that God no longer speaks *even though the Bible never says that he has stopped speaking to us*. I know one thing for certain; none of these authors or theologians has had the Lord confront them while they were mowing their lawn. A personal encounter with the Almighty tends to knock one's blinders off.

It is difficult for us to envision things that we have not experienced. God has to knock the scales off of our eyes in order for us to begin to see. The Israelites are not the only ones who can be described with the words, **"though seeing, they do not see, though hearing, they do not hear or understand" (Matthew 13:13).** We are all chained to our experience and find it difficult to see or hear things outside our experience. God has a habit of invading our lives and opening our minds to his possibilities. He has done this throughout history.

By the time God interrupted me in 1989, I had already preached a series of messages that outlined why he no longer speaks to us personally today. I had already constructed my fence around this truth using logical deductions rather than clear statements of scripture. I had built the fence of my theology and smugly locked the gate certain that God did not speak today. That is the way things would have remained if God had not impolitely careened through my fence and knocked a giant hole in it. As I later examined the wreckage in order to determine what had happened, I was able to see how illogical and unsound the whole construct really was. I found that I had built a theology to defend my experience of God's silence, rather than seeking to change my experience to align with God's Word. But I could not see that before he did me the favor of crashing through my presuppositions. By his grace he knocked my blinders off in such a radical way that I could not put them back on again.

Of course, this had implications for my continued tenure in the denomination that had nurtured me and that I loved. Within a couple of years, years in which I poured over the Scriptures on this topic, I realized that I could not stay in the denomination. I no longer agreed with them on this basic issue, and if I wanted to teach others what I believed, I had to separate from the denomination. This wasn't easy; I had grown up in this church body. I had learned to love my fellow pastors and the church leaders. I also deeply loved the people that God had brought to my congregation. But I realized I could not stay.

Leaving a Denomination

I didn't give any thought to taking the congregation with me when I decided it was time to leave. The leaders of our denomination taught us to believe that the people were the denomination's sheep. I had no thought of challenging this teaching. In fact, this was so much a part of my worldview, that when my congregation had added an associate pastor in 1991, I had specifically looked for someone to whom I could entrust the congregation should my departure become necessary. By the beginning of 1993, I knew that it was time to go.

I quietly began to make preparations to resign my position. Once I had resigned, I planned to move to another city across the United States where a friend of mine lived. I had begun to develop a business plan for a small company so that I would have an income. My friend and I thought that we could begin a home group, and see if it might eventually become a new church plant. Things were moving along according to plan, until the Lord's voice interrupted me again.

As with his first interruption, I remember where I was and what I was doing when the Lord intervened. I had just finished a telephone conversation with the man I was going to hire as my sales manager for the new business. We were putting the final touches on the compensations plans, and I ended the phone call feeling that everything was going exceedingly well. I was sitting in my church office, and had just put the phone down on my desk, when the jarring but wondrous voice of the Lord once again changed things. This

time he only spoke one sentence, "The good shepherd lays down his life for the sheep."

The first time that the Lord's voice broke into my conscious world, I had been indignant. This time, as he opened my mind to understand the nuances of his thought, I was humbled. I instantly knew that I had accepted a false premise. I had believed that the people of the congregation were the denomination's sheep. The Lord showed me that he had used me to call the people into relationship in the congregation. He had nurtured and raised them on my teaching. They were his sheep, but I was the assigned shepherd for this flock. He intervened because I was currently a good shepherd, but if I deserted the sheep, I would no longer be a good shepherd. He intervened so that I would not miss my calling in South Florida, and so that the congregation would not be harmed by my lack of understanding.

I was grateful that the Lord explained things to me before I had made any irreversible commitments. He saved me from making an enormous mistake, but he didn't save me from some difficult choices. I don't believe I can adequately convey the difficulty that confronted me after he intervened. I had decided to resign in order to keep the peace in my congregation and in my denomination. I wanted to avoid confrontation. After the Lord spoke to me, I knew my path could only lead to confrontation.

I now knew that I needed to prepare the congregation for a difficult and very public split with the denomination. I had no doubt that this path was filled with accusation, severed relationships, and many other difficulties. But I wanted to be a good shepherd; I shut down my business plans on that very day because I needed to give my full attention to this new direction.[1]

We finally left the denomination in the fall of 1994. That step was every bit as painful and difficult as I had imagined. But the Lord continued to grant us grace through the entire process. I wish that I could say that we left with good feelings on all sides, but that would not be accurate. We did not leave perfectly, and even if we had, the act of severing from a denomination is most always an emotionally ragged affair. But God's grace was there for my congregation and for the denomination, and he got us through this painful time.

---

[1] Although this sounds that I made the irrevocable decision to leave the denomination in 1993, I actually held out hope that the relationship could be saved. I was in the process of working with the denomination over several other areas of theology, and I hoped that I could persuade the leaders to take a fresh look at some of scriptures that I believed they had misapplied. I believed that if I could bring new light to minor issues, and they received it, that there was hope to tackle even more major issues. This hope proved futile, and we began to make preparations to leave in 1994.

Connecting with MorningStar

By the beginning of 1995, we were a newly independent congregation wondering what God had in store for us. We had a variety of challenges yet to overcome, but we felt a new freedom to follow the Lord's leading. We were eager to pursue him. We were also eager to connect with some organization or denomination what would provide new relationship, and would help us grow into the things of the Lord.

A friend had introduced me to MorningStar Ministries and Rick Joyner's teachings prior to our departure from the denomination. I had begun to read *The MorningStar Journal* and many of Rick's books, and realized that many of the things that I had learned in my study of the Bible, were truths that Rick also affirmed. As I read Rick's material, I began to believe that we were working from the same biblical outline, but I recognized that his outline was more detailed than mine. So I began to explore the possibility of a relationship with MorningStar.

In May of 1995, Dawn and I rented a camper, packed up our growing family, and travelled to Fort Mill, South Carolina to experience a MorningStar conference together. I had attended some conferences in 1994 without Dawn, and I wanted to introduce her to this ministry. I was excited about the biblical integrity that the MorningStar leaders displayed, and the clear desire to pursue the Lord with all their might. I wanted Dawn to be as excited as I was about MorningStar. I wanted her to see what I saw in this ministry.

When we arrived, I registered my family and received the introductory packet of materials for the conference. While reading through the material, I discovered a theological glitch that I had not expected to discover in MorningStar's material. I was disturbed by it, but it didn't diminish my interest in the ministry. I deemed it an obvious enough problem that I suspected the Lord could easily correct it.

In my 1989 encounter with the Lord, he had challenged me to study what the Bible said about finances and giving. After five years of study, and having written a stewardship program, I was pretty confident that I understood some basic principles about giving. One of those basic principles is that God wants people to give to him freely. That means that we must do what we can to stay away from manipulation in order that people can give freely and without compulsion. I had noted a growing trend in Christian ministries to violate this basic principle. Many ministries were beginning to manipulate the people who supported them by giving incentives if they gave a certain amount of money. Some ministries were giving away items; some were giving away elite status. But it all becomes a subtle manipulation intended to get donors to give more money to the ministry. This type of giving is not about freedom. It is about manipulation and compulsion.

When I opened up the packet of MorningStar materials, I saw that MorningStar had now done the same thing. They offered status incentives for those who became financial supporters of the ministry. If you gave a certain amount each year, you could become a silver eagle, and if you gave more, you could become a gold eagle giver. I don't remember what benefits were offered, or even what other levels there were. I recognized that this was a departure for this ministry, and it grieved me. I really wanted to connect to MorningStar, but I also wanted to connect to a ministry from which I could

learn. I didn't want to begin a relationship with disagreement over such a basic issue.

I am relating this story to show how firmly God connected me to MorningStar Ministries and Rick Joyner, not to discredit ministries who use this type of giving procedure. I am sharing what I understand the Bible to say, and how important it is to me. Because when the conference started, God used this very issue to endear my heart to Rick Joyner.

When the conference opened on Thursday morning, and Rick stepped up to speak, the last thing I expected was any discussion of the giving brochure that had bothered me. Yet this is exactly where Rick started. He publicly repented for the brochure, and explained that he had written it while he was jet-lagged and dealing with too much or too little caffeine (I can't remember which). He clearly repudiated the brochure and explained that it did not reflect God's heart on the matter.

I sat in the audience awestruck. I had never seen such integrity on display in such a public forum. I was enthralled by the humility Rick displayed as he explained his mistake. At that point, I was hooked. I wanted more of this type of leadership and the life that flowed from it. It was as if God had engineered this whole episode so that I could see into Rick's heart in a way that would normally have taken years of relationship. In that moment, I was absolutely certain that this was the place for our congregation.

We soon connected with MorningStar through the MorningStar Fellowship of Ministries (MFM), and several years later we became the first MorningStar Fellowship Church (MFC). This connection played a major role when God began to speak to us about an approaching storm. He was connecting us so that we had mature guidance when he spoke to us about Satan's plans for South Florida.

3

NEW DAWN

Preparing For A New Dawn

MorningStar Ministries became an important part of our growth and development in the years immediately after our departure from our former denomination. MorningStar's influence in our congregation's life began in earnest at that conference in May of 1995. God used that conference to initiate a major change in our congregation.

The conference had started on Thursday morning, but because we had young children with us, Dawn and I could not always be in the meetings together. However, on Friday night, Dawn and I were able to attend the session together. Thousands of people were packed into the auditorium on that evening. A highly regarded prophetic minister was scheduled to speak, and the atmosphere was electric with expectation. We were caught up in the excitement, but did not really understand its source. As the night wore on, we began to understand.

Near the end of the meeting, the prophetic minister began to prophesy over some of the people in the audience. He called people out of the audience by name, and gave them insight or encouragement from the Lord. We were surprised by how much detail the speaker shared about the lives of these people he did not know. We had seen public ministry of this type before, but never at this level of specific detail. The thousands of us who were gathered in that auditorium knew that the Lord was pouring out something special. It quickly became something even more special for Dawn and I.

As I think back on the moment that the speaker called out our names, I am still a little awed. Thousands of people were attending this conference. We knew no one. Yet the Lord decided to use the prophetic minister to give us an important message. He said, "Randal and Dawn, there is a new dawn."

Dawn and I were so taken aback by being addressed, we didn't know what to do. We asked the people seated near us for help. When they found out that we were the Randal and Dawn who had been called, they told us that we had been told to come to the front of the auditorium. So we walked to the front, and those who were ministering prayed for us and encouraged us.

We did not have much of an idea what the speaker meant by saying that there was a new dawn. We did know that he had referred to Isaiah 60:1-3, but we did not know much else. Isaiah 60:1-3 states,

> **"Arise, shine, for your light has come, and the glory of the LORD rises upon you. See, darkness covers the earth and thick darkness is over the peoples, but the LORD rises upon you and his glory appears over you. Nations will come to**

**your light, and kings to the brightness of
your dawn."**

We understood that the new dawn had something to do with
Isaiah 60, and that this new dawn would be a marker
indicating that Isaiah 60 was coming to pass, but we did not
know much else. We knew God had given us direction, we
just didn't know how to read the map yet. We didn't have to
wait very long before the Lord sent someone to help us read
it.

We left that conference convinced that we had found our
new ministry home, and excited for the future. We certainly
did not understand all the things that the Lord was doing, but
we knew he was up to something. We felt like we were
launching into something new with the Lord.

When we got back to Coral Springs, we soon began to
wonder if our launch had been aborted. Within weeks of
returning home, our congregation began to go through a
sifting. I had been excitedly charging forward following the
direction that I believed God's Spirit was leading. I had
assumed that our entire congregation felt the same way. I was
wrong.

Several of our leaders began to question our direction and
focus. This cost us a great deal of momentum, and eventually
a number of families left the congregation. As I look back, I
can see that the Lord was clarifying our vision and focus.
However, when you are going through it, it is wrenching and
disheartening. Since I could still hear the echoes of my 1989
encounter with the Lord, I didn't whine about it. I knew I
needed to take what responsibility I could for any leadership
errors, and move on from there. But as a result of this "bump

in the road," our congregation lost just enough members to stretch our budget to the breaking point. Our future was not looking good. We did not understand how the Lord was preparing a new dawn.

Just at that difficult juncture, a group of leaders from another congregation in our city approached us and told us that they were considering disbanding their congregation. We had worked with this congregation during the previous years on an effective youth outreach ministry in our city. As a result, we had a good relationship with them. Their pastor had resigned because of moral failure about six months earlier. Since then, the remaining leaders had labored tirelessly to keep things going, but they were being worn ragged.

When they approached us, I felt one of those now familiar nudges from the Lord that led me to do something about the situation. I knew this was a good congregation. They were from a Pentecostal background, but had pursued independence from their denomination because of certain doctrinal disagreements. I knew that we were compatible at many levels, and felt we could work through the areas where we did not mesh that well. So rather than agree that it might be good for them to disband, I broached the topic of a merger. They were pleased by the idea, and quickly warmed to it.

Anyone that has ever done a study of church mergers knows that there is a right way to merge two churches, and there is a wrong way to merge two churches. Those who have done such studies would necessarily have concluded that ours was the wrong way to merge a church. First, this should be a slow and deliberate process. We moved quickly to schedule a "worship together date" for the last Sunday in July, only weeks later. Second, surveys and studies should be done to make certain that congregational expectations and leadership styles are merged in the best possible way. Discussions need to center on the many needs of a merged congregation in order to plan for a smooth transition. We did some of this, but we took a couple weeks to discuss things that should have taken a year. While our merger was not the most ill-conceived idea in the history of the modern church, I believe that it should at least receive honorable mention.

It is easy to understand how bad an idea this was in hindsight. We were a people forged through the unifying fire of departing from a denomination. On top of that, our congregation had just gone through the stress of seeing a number of people leave because of doctrinal disagreement. Those who remained were true believers in our mission and purpose, and would not be moved from that path. Of course, the other congregation had also gone through the same unifying fire as they had departed from their denomination, and the public fall of their pastor had unified those who remained around their core values and purpose. We wanted to merge the hardcore survivors from two different ministry streams into something new. What could go wrong?

The answer, of course, is that a lot could go wrong. The recipe for conflict was built into both congregations' DNA. When you factor in the fact that the leadership of the other congregation was exhausted, that they had been through indescribable emotional turmoil and pain even as they had faithfully carried out their duties, you can't imagine that a merger would work. Red flags of warning were waving over this merger idea from the very beginning. In retrospect, it is hard to imagine how this could have been part of God's "new dawn." However, the Lord had some surprises in store.

God Forges A New Dawn

Our congregations met together to worship on the last Sunday of July, 1995. The worship hall was filled with excitement at the possibility of what could happen. People from both congregations came early to see if God was up to something. I don't think that many us understood just how audacious we were being, but that was probably a good thing.

We came together on that Sunday not quite knowing what to expect. We had called it a "worship date," but we had no clear plan on how to determine if this date should become a marriage. We didn't appreciate just how much the divine matchmaker was working behind the scenes, and how obvious he was about to make things.

The Lord helped things along by bringing a prophetic minister to our meeting that day. We had not met the man before this, and he did not know us. He was from the western United States, and had received his training from some notable prophetic ministries there. He had come to our city for business, and just happened to come to our meeting on that Sunday morning. He was a veteran of prophetic ministry who understood congregational life and protocol. When he came into our meeting, and the worship started, the Lord began to speak to him about his purposes for us. He quickly wrote everything down on several pieces of paper, and handed the papers to one of our leaders before the praise songs had ended. He was making certain that it would be apparent to everyone that what he had written was not influenced by anything said or discussed in the meeting.

Since I would be the pastor of a merged congregation, I was scheduled to speak that morning. I shared a bit about what God had been doing at my congregation. As part of the message, I told everyone about the May conference, and how we were checking to see if this merger was the "new dawn" that God had promised. I shared Isaiah 60, and painted a vision of a congregation formed by God as a sign that his purposes in Isaiah 60 were being fulfilled.

At the conclusion of my message, the prophetic minister excitedly asked one of our leaders if he could speak to me. That leader brought him to me and introduced him. They briefly explained about the notes that he had written during the praise songs, and told me I would want to see what was in the notes. When I saw some of the things, I asked the prophetic minister to read the notes to the congregation. He shared several things, but one thing he had written that day deserves special mention. He read from his paper, "The new dawn is here. Isaiah 60—Arise shine for thy light has come, and the glory of the Lord is risen in this place."

We had our new dawn. While the idea to merge the two congregations did not appear the smartest thing to do, God sealed it in such a profound way that we could not deny his hand. New Dawn Community Church came into existence three weekends later, on the third Sunday of August, 1995.

Even with such a prophetic start, we still experienced the normal bumps and bruises that are common to such mergers, but the fact that God had so obviously confirmed our merger helped us immensely. We were launching into our new dawn.

The prophetic minister said many things on that Sunday morning he was with us. One thing he said did not mean much to us then, but it certainly makes sense now. He said,

"The Lord said that you are going to take this area by storm." With those words, the Lord foreshadowed a bit of our calling and purpose as we entered into his new dawn.

God had prepared a teacher. Now he brought a new congregation into existence in order to carry out his purposes. The Lord was forming a team that he would use to preserve many lives. We didn't know any of this yet, but he really was going to use us to take the area *by storm*.

4

STORM WARNINGS

For the next three years after New Dawn was formed, the Lord molded us into a team. He took the members of two very different congregations and melded us together so that we could have common vision. This did not happen without the normal stress and tension of congregational life, but it did happen.

We were approaching our third anniversary as a congregation when the Lord once again intervened in a way that changed everything. This time, he not only changed how we viewed ourselves, but also how we used our authority on the earth. We knew he had given his Church the keys of the Kingdom of Heaven, but like most Christians, we didn't understand the vast authority he intended to give us through those keys. So he began to teach us.

This storm odyssey began with a dream. Those of us who are familiar with the Bible realize that dreams are one of the Lord's favorite forms of communications. That doesn't mean that every dream is from the Lord. In fact, many dreams simply process the stresses of the day. Even so, the Lord still uses this form of revelation to communicate to his people.

Since dreams are often metaphors, they need to be interpreted. Both Joseph and Daniel needed to interpret dreams for other people. In the same way, God's people who have the spiritual gift of interpretation are able to help interpret the dreams of those who receive them today. Because we were convinced that God still speaks through dreams, we worked diligently to understand them. In those first three years after we formed New Dawn, God developed the gift of interpretation in our midst, so that we would be prepared to take our area by storm.

The Dreams

During the early morning hours of August 11, 1998, I had a vivid dream. It was so vivid that I can clearly remember it today. In the dream, Dawn and I were standing outside of our home. As I looked around, I saw that the sky was filled with gray storm clouds. I knew that the clouds were from an approaching hurricane. We had to decide whether to close and lock our hurricane shutters or not. I had a strong conviction that this hurricane was not going to hit, even though the forecasters insisted that it would. In the end, I closed the shutters out of prudence rather than conviction. I didn't believe that this storm was going to hit us. However, I was convinced that there really was a hurricane coming to the Fort Lauderdale area.

When I awoke from the dream, I strongly suspected that the dream had not been symbolic. I was certain that the dream was about two literal hurricanes. The first hurricane would appear such a threat that the weather forecasters would advise us to prepare for it. However, this first storm would not hit our area. But there was another storm coming that would hit our area.

I was so disturbed by the vividness of this dream, that I didn't attempt to fall back to sleep. Instead I got up to seek the Lord about the dream. As I sought him, he gave me confirmation that the dream was about literal hurricanes. Since that was all the information I had, and it wasn't much, I asked the Lord to provide more information. I knew that if this were important, he would certainly show us more.

By 1998, we had lived in South Florida for over a decade. Even though the Miami area just to our south had witnessed Hurricane Andrew's ferocity back in 1992, we still didn't view hurricanes as much of a threat. We just did not see many of them. Of course, that would change during the next decade as storms such as Charlie, Ivan, Jeanne, Dennis, Katrina, Rita, and Wilma taught us a newfound respect. But back in 1998, the Lord not only had to send us a warning about a hurricane, he had to educate us about why this warning was important.

He continued that education on August 20th, 1998, just nine days after I had asked him for more insight into what he was telling us about hurricanes. On that day, a tropical storm named Bonnie formed in the Atlantic Ocean. Also on that day, the Lord gave Dawn a dream about the two hurricanes that he had shown to me. She didn't realize that she had dreamed about two hurricanes. She thought she had dreamed about her two sisters.

Dawn's two sisters are Bonnie and Irene. Both of Dawn's sisters live in the Midwest. Dawn dreamed that her sister Bonnie was going to come for a visit. However, at the last minute she could not come. Instead, Dawn's sister Irene came to visit by surprise.

31

There was a bit more to[1] the dream than this, but I've captured the pertinent points. As Dawn told me the dream, I understood parts of what it meant. I knew that a storm named Bonnie had just developed in the Atlantic. The National Hurricane Center had begun providing alerts, and the news stations were urging Floridians to pay close attention to this storm. Based upon Dawn's dream, I concluded that it might appear that tropical storm Bonnie wanted to visit, but that it would not. I did not have a lot of time to do further interpretation, since I was in North Carolina at a conference when she told me the dream. I simply told her to tell the congregation that Bonnie might threaten South Florida, but it would not hit us.

We didn't realize the significance of this bit of information until several days later. By then, tropical storm Bonnie had become a hurricane, and had swelled to monstrous proportions. As it began to meander close to Florida, South Florida's population began to get nervous. Because of Dawn's dream, we were able to encourage our congregation and tell them that we did not believe this storm would hit us. Of course, we also encouraged them to be prepared in case we misunderstood the meaning of the dream. When Bonnie turned away from us, we rejoiced that we had understood the dream correctly, and we took one step closer to understanding what God was saying to us about the storm that would hit.

Since Hurricane Bonnie had looked like she wanted to come for a visit, but she had not, we realized that we needed to understand the rest of Dawn's dream. Was there an Irene in our near future?

The National Hurricane Center posts the list of future hurricane names on its web page. I didn't realize this at first, but as I began to research the rest of Dawn's dream, I found that list of names. As I looked through the names scheduled for 1998 storms, I was relieved to see that there was no Irene. I didn't quite know what the rest of Dawn's dream might mean, but I realized it did not mean that we would see a storm named Irene in 1998.

As I left the list of 1998 storm names, I noticed that there was also a list for 1999. When I checked this list, I was less than happy to find out that there was an Irene in the list for 1999. Based upon my understanding of the two dreams so far, I was almost certain that there would be a Hurricane Irene in 1999. I also knew that it would visit our area unexpectedly, since Dawn's sister of the same name had visited unexpectedly in her dream.

Since God was directing my attention to it a year in advance, I knew we had time to gather more information. Even though I believed that I had found a significant piece of information, and even though I believed that the Lord might be warning us that a hurricane named Irene could be hitting us by surprise in 1999, I didn't tell anyone. I didn't believe I had enough information to do much about it. Both dreams had spoken in a way that let me know that a first storm would miss, and a second storm would hit. Dawn's dream had given me a name, and the National Hurricane Center directed me to the year for that second storm. But I needed a lot more than this in order to do something about it. So I began to ask the Lord to give us more information, and without telling my congregation why, I asked them to forward any dreams that might have to do with storms. I was hoping that the Lord would speak to some of our congregation members in order to give us more clarity. He met that hope beyond all my expectations.

The Lord began to pour out many dreams to the members of our congregation. On October 2, 1998, a twelve-year-old member of our congregation had an amazing dream. She did not know that we were seeking information about storms, but when she told her mother the dream, her mother forwarded it to me.

In the dream, the young lady and a friend were walking along a road in Deerfield Beach, a small city in the northeast corner of Broward County about ten miles to the northeast of our city. As she and her friend were walking, they surveyed the damage that a hurricane had done to that area. They saw many houses that were torn apart. Everywhere they walked they saw extreme damage. As they passed a hotel near the ocean, they saw beds and other things from the hotel in the street and on the beach. The damage was overwhelming.

When they walked back to the friend's home, she noted that it was painted yellow, a strange detail since her friend's home was not yellow in waking life. More importantly, she also noted that her friend's father was watching the news on a battery operated portable television set. The news was filled with reports of the hurricane. It had hit Broward County by surprise as a category four storm. The news reported that wind speeds had gusted to almost two hundred miles per hour and had caused severe damage across the area.

As I read this dream, I was stunned by the description of the storm, and by the fact that it confirmed that the storm would hit by surprise. I instantly understood why the Lord was directing our attention to Irene. I've used the word catastrophe to describe this storm because that is exactly what a storm like this would be. If a storm of category four magnitude struck by surprise, the damage would be unimaginable. The death toll would be unthinkable. According to the Saffir-Simpson hurricane scale, a category four hurricane has sustained winds of 130 to 156 miles per hour. The hurricane center helpfully describes what a category four hurricane can be expected to do:

Catastrophic damage will occur

There is a very high risk of injury or death to people, livestock, and pets due to flying and falling debris. Nearly all older (pre-1994) mobile homes will be destroyed. A high percentage of newer mobile homes also will be destroyed. Poorly constructed homes can sustain complete collapse of all walls as well as the loss of the roof structure. Well-built homes also can sustain severe damage with loss of most of the roof structure and/or some exterior walls. Extensive damage to roof coverings, windows, and doors will occur. Large amounts of windborne debris will be lofted into the air. Windborne debris damage will break most unprotected windows and penetrate some protected windows. There will be a high percentage of structural damage to the top floors of apartment buildings. Steel frames in older industrial buildings can collapse. There will be a high percentage of collapse to older unreinforced masonry buildings. Most windows will be blown out of high-rise buildings resulting in falling glass, which will pose a threat for days to weeks after the storm. Nearly all commercial signage, fences, and canopies will be destroyed. Most trees will be snapped or uprooted and power poles downed. Fallen trees and power poles will isolate residential areas. Power outages will last for weeks to possibly months. Long-term water shortages will increase human suffering. Most of the area will be uninhabitable for weeks or months.

I remember reading that description several times trying to comprehend what would happen to heavily populated Broward and Palm Beach counties. I couldn't imagine a storm of this magnitude hitting our area at all, much less by surprise. When a category four storm hits an area that is expecting to be hit it, the results are calamitous. What would happen if virtually no one prepared? I could only shudder at the thought. I realized that the damage that the young lady described in her dream was exactly the type of damage a category four storm would do. I knew that the Lord was giving me the details I had asked him to give.

I now knew that Deerfield Beach was ground zero for the most damage from this storm. Since a hurricane is not a small event, I realized that wide areas of Broward and Palm Beach counties were at major risk. But I also realized that Deerfield would be the most damaged.

This also explained a part of Dawn's dream that I have not mentioned. In Dawn's dream, Irene brought deer steak when she visited. I know that most people call deer steak venison, however, in the dream it was specifically deer steak. I didn't understand why Irene brought deer steak until I read this young lady's dream. I realized that it was a grim reminder that this hurricane would slaughter *Deer*-field. It was one more way that the Lord let us know how serious this was.

5

ENGAGING THE STORM

Alerting the Troops

The Lord gave several other dreams to members and friends of our congregation over the next months that confirmed the things that we already knew about this storm. By this time, I was absolutely convinced that a hurricane named Irene was going to hit us in 1999. The Lord continued to confirm this in a variety of ways. We found out later, with some level of surprise, that the date that I had the first dream (August 11) was the birthday of Dawn's sister, Irene. We viewed such "coincidences" as further confirmation of the things that the Lord was communicating to us about this monster storm.

As a pastor in Broward County, I realized that I could not keep this information to myself. I had relationship with many other pastors in Broward County, and I wanted to inform them of what the Lord was showing us. I received permission to share at our November pastor's meeting. On November 4, 1998, I marshaled the facts that the Lord had given to us, and informed this gathering of what we faced in 1999. I didn't attempt to rally them behind what God was showing to us. I was submitting it to them for judgment. I wanted their input on the things that the Lord was showing us.

I was impressed that they did not dismiss the whole thing out of hand. Over the years, each of us had received our share of hurricane "prophecies" from folks. In every case that I remember, those supposed prophecies were generic to the point of being almost impossible to rationally consider. What I presented was far different. I was able to share about a half dozen dreams that confirmed one another. Since I had not yet told the congregation what God had shown to us, there was no possibility of cross-contamination, or that people were having anxiety dreams based upon things they were hearing. I met and dealt with most of the obvious objections from the pastors. I was eager to see how these men whom I respected would respond.

When the group listened politely to my presentation, I was pleased. When several of the pastors asked good questions, I was very pleased. I believed we had achieved an important victory. Although the group, as a whole, did not get involved any further, I did receive encouragement and support from enough of them as individuals to have made the effort worthwhile. I also believed that we had achieved something of value, in that the majority of the group had adopted a wait-and-see attitude, rather than rejecting the matter out-of-hand. I did not expect more. None of us had ever dealt with something like this. We had no precedence to guide us. In spite of this, they handled the matter with maturity and tact.

Since I was connected to MorningStar Ministries, I also submitted our conclusions about Irene to them. I knew that as a international prophetic organization, they could have encountered this type of thing before, and could have some insights that would help us. Steve Thompson was vice-president of MorningStar at the time. He has a keen mind and good prophetic understanding. When he read what God had given us, he confirmed that the Lord was speaking to us, and that we were interpreting it correctly. He also encouraged us to keep pursuing the Lord on the topic.

This was an important contact. Up until that time I had no idea what to do with this information. I couldn't imagine prophesying it in order to warn people. I knew very few people would listen, even in the Church. We simply didn't have much of a grid for dealing with something like this in South Florida. However, Steve remind me that one of the main purposes of the prophetic was to marshal prayer against the disasters the Lord might reveal to us. Since the Lord had shown Irene to us, we concluded that he wanted us to call the churches of South Florida together to pray against this storm. Even though we realized that few churches would respond, we were confident that the Lord would bring enough of the Church together to do the job of protecting South Florida. Rather than looking ahead to the end of 1999 with trepidation, we realized that the Lord had enlisted us to make a difference on behalf of South Florida.

The Intercessory Call

It was vitally important that we understood our intercessory role, and the authority that our Savior had won for us. It is also vitally important in the days ahead that we understand those same things. God has called his prophetic people as intercessors to stand in the gap for their regions. The Lord had told Ezekiel, "**I looked for a man among them who**

would build up the wall and stand before me in the gap on behalf of the land so I would not have to destroy it, but I found none" (Ezekiel 22:30). God has never stopped looking for people to stand in the gap. He is looking for those who will pray on behalf of their respective geographic areas, releasing his mercy and grace as necessary. Just as Jesus calmed the storms, so his people have been given authority to calm the storms and natural disasters that beset this world. Jesus has given his Church the keys to the Kingdom. He told Peter, **"I will give you the keys of the kingdom of heaven; whatever you bind on earth will be bound in heaven, and whatever you loose on earth will be loosed in heaven" (Matthew 16:18).** When Jesus ascended into heaven, he gave gifts to men. The keys of authority were included in those gifts. When he calls us to defend an area, he makes certain we have the authority and power to protect that area.

One of the great questions asked after tragic natural disasters inevitably is, "Where was God?" I can virtually guarantee that question would have been asked in South Florida if Irene had hit by surprise as a category four storm. When disaster hits, it is human nature to survey the damage and ask after God. I suspect in most cases, he was there, but he could not find someone to stand in the gap with understanding. As a result, the disaster could not be averted.

The Lord is diligent about seeking those who will stand in the gap. He once called us to pray against a winter storm that was going to hit the northeast coast of the United States. It is not an easy task to mobilize South Floridians to pray against a winter storm even while they are basking in beautiful weather. But the Lord called us to do it. He specifically told us that he could not find anyone who would pray against the storm. He was looking for someone to stand in the gap, but could not find anyone in that geographic area, so he offered the opportunity to us. That incident taught me about just how diligently our God seeks for those who will stand in the gap. I believe he is always looking for someone to stand in the gap in order to avert tragedy, but we may have a hard time hearing that call.

Does this mean that every natural disaster is avoidable? I believe that many are avoidable. I believe we have far more authority than we think. Psalm 115 tells us, **"The highest heavens belong to the LORD, but the earth he has given to man" (Psalm 115:16).** When God created this earth, he gave Adam authority over it. Adam lost it to Satan. Jesus won it back, and he has given those keys of authority to his Church. When we use the keys, good things happen and disaster is averted. When we do not use the keys, bad things happen.

Of course, that doesn't mean that we can avoid every disaster. World history is about birth pains. The Bible clearly teaches that birth pains—natural disasters—must increase as the world wears down. However, even when natural disasters are unavoidable, we can use the keys to release protection for all those who are in harms way. We must take our job seriously, not only for the Church, but also because God doesn't delight in the death of the wicked (see Ezekiel 33:11). If God doesn't like it when the wicked are killed by natural disasters, how much must he grieve when such things harm children and other innocents? He intends to release his protection through his Church. If we are not doing our job, tragedy is multiplied. When we do our job, lives are preserved.

Our congregation has learned a lot about this since 1998. However, when we first learned about Irene, we were stepping into new territory, and didn't understand the fullness of our intercessory role. God would teach us through Irene, and he would use us many more times in the years to come to release protection to our area. But in 1998 we were taking fledgling steps.

Rallying the Troops

The Lord had shown us Irene. We knew that he does not rejoice when people perish, so we concluded that he had not shown us Irene to show us inevitable disaster. He showed us Irene so that his love for people could be manifest, and so that people would not perish. He showed us it so that we could bind it on earth in the same way that its death and destruction were bound in heaven. We knew what we needed to do, so we began to rally the Church in Broward County to help us.

I started with my own congregation. On a Sunday morning in January 1999, I began to unfold what God had shown us, and what role God had outlined for us. As I have previously mentioned, the Lord had prepared our congregation to step into this role. He had made us into a team. He now gave us vision for the things that needed to be done. We stepped into this mantle and began to pray against this storm. We also realized that we needed to have joint meetings with other congregations across Broward County.

To that end, I began to inform other congregations on March 1, 1999. We planned our first multi-congregation prayer meeting about Hurricane Irene on March 21, 1999. I invited just over fifty Broward congregations to participate with us. I had written out what I believed God was showing us, and I shared how he had shown it to us (see Appendix 1). We had decided to send the invitation out by mail and facsimiles. We asked each church to join us for a special worship service and prayer meeting. Our purpose was to explain the threat, and to pray against it.

I invited churches from all sorts of denominations, from all spectrums of Christianity. Even if they did not respond, I hoped that there would be those in their midst who would respond by praying as individuals. I also, by clear example, wanted to inform these churches that God still loved and cared for his people, and was willing to communicate to protect us. I knew we had been called to take the area by storm, and I wanted to demonstrate God's plan to as many of his people as I could.

Even though I had all these noble aspirations, I still paused before I sent the fax on that March day in 1999. I remember specifically thinking about my reputation. I realized I was sending this note out to people who knew me, and some of them even respected me. I wondered what this would do to my reputation. At that moment, the Lord nudged me in a way that made me laugh. He showed me that I really had not built much of a reputation. It is pretty difficult to damage something that you don't really have. The logic and humor of that moment overcame any reticence. I pressed the key that sent all the facsimiles on their way.

Storming the Walls of Heaven

We had chosen to have the first joint prayer meeting at Good News Church in central Broward County. Good News Church had a much larger worship hall than we did, and because of its central location, it was far easier for most people to get to it. The pastor and leaders of Good News had graciously offered the use of their building. Their pastor at the time, Bob Sutton, had been in the pastors' meeting in November, and had immediately recognized that the Lord was trying to help Broward County. His congregation eagerly stepped forward and became our prayer partners throughout 1999.

About a half dozen churches were represented at that March meeting. We were excited that they responded to our invitation. We knew the mountain of skepticism that we had to climb in order to convince anyone to come to a meeting like this. First, they had to scale the wall of unbelief in order to believe that God had actually communicated to us. Then, if that wasn't difficult enough, they had to swallow the fact that a hurricane could hit by surprise.

For those of us who are familiar with the National Hurricane Center, and how well it forecasts storm tracks, this may have been one of the more difficult things to apprehend. The Hurricane Center posts watches and warnings over areas, depending on the variables in a hurricane's track. I believed that the Lord was showing us that the National Hurricane Center would be so wrong about Irene's track, that they would not post a hurricane warning for our area. That sort of thing just didn't happen. The Hurricane Center is usually able to respond to changing circumstances, and post warnings quickly if things change. I knew that Irene would break that mold. It would hit by surprise. A surprising number of congregations and their leaders were able to get beyond this difficult claim in order to come together and pray.

During that meeting, we recounted what the Lord had shown to us, explained the biblical basis for our response, and rallied the troops for an assault on this storm named Irene. After this, we prayed with faith and excitement over the invitation that God had given to us. We felt the presence of God, and his pleasure as we prayed. He had looked for someone to stand in the gap, and we had responded. It was a great night in South Florida.

We held several other joint prayer meetings throughout the rest of the year. Each one of them felt powerful and effective. Even then, most congregations did not limit their prayer to just those meetings. They prayed throughout that year. At New Dawn we prayed at virtually every meeting of our congregation. We didn't pray for long period of time every time, but we prayed fervently.

Checking In Along The Way

By the time we started the hurricane season on June 1 of that year, we had begun to wonder if our prayers were having an impact. We wanted to know if we were reducing the storm's strength. We wanted to know if we were still under the same threat that we had initially seen, or if the gap had been filled to some point. The Lord graciously responded to that desire by giving one of our members another dream.

In this dream, that member of our congregation was standing in a field next to a wooded area. An arrow flew by him so near, that he could hear the sound. Suddenly, a deer ran from the wooded area with an arrow in it. It ran into the field and stopped. A woman came running out of the wooded area after the deer. The woman was wearing hunting clothes and looked like Dawn. She had fitted another arrow to her bow, and took aim at the deer again. But just then, a group of people gathered around the deer and began helping it. Since the woman no longer had a shot, she put down the bow and walked away. There was one person in the group protecting the deer, whom the man recognized. His name was Adam.

When I received this dream, I understood its incredible message immediately. The deer in the field, of course, represented Deerfield Beach. I also knew that Dawn and her older sister, Irene, have a striking resemblance to one another. So I knew that the woman represented Hurricane Irene. I also knew that the group of people who had stopped the woman from shooting the deer represented those who were standing in the gap for our area against Irene. They were the sons and daughters of Adam who had taken the authority that Christ had extended to them.

As I pondered this dream, I realized that we were no longer facing a catastrophe. In retrospect, I believe that the one arrow that hit the deer probably represented a category one storm. But at that time, I did not understand it. I did understand that the dream was showing us that we had reduced the strength of the storm significantly.

This dream revitalized our prayers. The Lord has sent us an encouragement. We knew we were having an effect, and we pressed forward with renewed fervor.

6

VICTORY OVER THE STORM

Faith Building

Two more things happened during the summer of 1999 that stoked the flames of our faith and increased our intensity. The first event was fairly mundane. The Deerfield family, the one that had made an appearance in the twelve-year-old girl's dream about Hurricane Irene, painted their house yellow. You will recall that strange detail of the young lady's dream. She didn't understand why the house was yellow in her dream, since it wasn't yellow in waking life. When she had asked her mother about it, her mother did not have an answer; neither did I. Then, nine months later, the family painted the house yellow.

You cannot imagine how this minor detail felt to us. Although we had met some level of skepticism about Irene as we had called people to pray, this type of detail encouraged us. The Lord used such minor details to show us that he was speaking clearly to us. This was just one more way he showed us the accuracy of the dreams. We were even more excited and amazed by what he was doing.

The second encouraging event involved a movie. It was one of the more bizarre ways that the Lord encouraged us that summer. He used the *The Addams Family* movie. Even though the movie was released in 1991, the SyFy channel was running it periodically that summer. I believe it was toward the end of summer when several members of the congregation had come across a scene from *The Addams Family* that had amazed them. I had never watched the movie; I wasn't really interested in macabre humor. Obviously, the Lord wasn't as stuffy as me.

The scene from the movie involved Uncle Fester reaching for a particular book on his library shelf. The name of the book comes into sharp focus as he reaches for it. Its name was *Hurricane Irene: Nightmare from Above*. After Uncle Fester takes the book off the shelf, he opens the book and releases Hurricane Irene into the environment.

You just cannot make this stuff up. I have to admit that by this time we were so caught up in all of this, my sense of discernment about what other people could swallow wasn't operating at a very high level. I actually shared this information in one of our prayer alerts. In retrospect, I'm sure that was a bad idea, even though at the time it seemed like the right thing to do. While it seems pretty funny now, I can't even begin to imagine what some of the pastors who received our prayer alerts thought about this bit of information. I'm sure it stretched them. I'm also sure it wasn't the wisest piece of information to include in a prayer alert.

Why was this such an important piece of information for us? In the dream about a deer wounded in a field, Adam was among the group of intercessors that protected the deer. We believed that it was a clear message that the second Adam's family was protecting that deer. Not only did The *Addam's Family* movie feature hurricane Irene, we also recognized a play on words that tied the movie to the dream. By itself, it wouldn't have meant much, but together with everything else God was doing, it was an interesting and unusual bit of affirmation.

The Media Gets Involved

I had purposely chosen not to include the churches of Palm Beach County in our prayer alerts. Even though Palm Beach County begins just to the north of Deerfield Beach, I had not felt a need to include them. This choice may have been incorrect, but the Lord has a way of fixing our mistakes.

During the summer of 1999, a news reporter from an NBC affiliate in West Palm Beach got wind of what was happening in Broward County. I didn't realize that we had stirred things up quite so much, but we had been loud enough that it caught his attention. The reporter, Jim Wicks, contacted me during the summer, and began to pursue this story. He wanted to interview me as part of a news story on what we were doing, and then broadcast the story of Hurricane Irene. In retrospect, I believe this was the Lord's way of sending a late invitation to the churches in Palm Beach County, even though I had not done so.

I finally granted the interview in September 1999. Jim did a wonderful job of interviewing me. He admitted later that he had approached the story with a great deal of skepticism, and initially had intended to portray us as more than a bit off the beam. But while he investigated the story, he became convinced that we were sincere, and that there was a good possibility that we were right. So when he did the interview, he crafted it in a way that invited people to join with me in prayer for our area. It was truly a remarkable moment as God used an NBC affiliate to get the information out to Palm Beach County.

That interview aired on October 1, 1999 to the Palm Beach County market. This was before Hurricane Irene formed. I was able to tape the broadcast on VHS tape, though the quality was hazy. Later, Jim gave me a copy of his footage so that I have a clear copy of that part of the broadcast. You can still see the interview at hurricaneirene.com, or on YouTube by doing a search for "Hurricane Irene God Does Speak."

I am also aware of the other reason that the Lord wanted this broadcast on the NBC affiliate. It has become an indisputable witness to the veracity of the facts that I am presenting. I am not just saying these things happened. We not only have the testimony of the dozens of pastors in our area who were impacted in one way or another, we also have video evidence. God does speak to his people.

The Storm

Twelve days after our prediction aired on the news, on October 13, 1999, Tropical Storm Irene formed. The storm formed southwest of Florida in the Caribbean. From the very beginning, the National Hurricane Center believed the storm would turn northwestward and curve out into the Gulf of Mexico. This became the monotonous and repeated forecast track during every hurricane update. Of course, the National Hurricane Center was wrong.

From a point just south of Cuba, Tropical Storm Irene moved inexorably northeastward toward the southeast portion of Florida. It crossed Cuba and began to gain strength as it moved across the Florida Straits. It became Hurricane Irene at this point. When Irene made landfall, it had the coldest temperature at its top that had been recorded to that time. That indicates that the storm was trying to develop. I have since learned that if Irene had spent as little as a few more hours over open water, in other words, if it had slowed down at all between Cuba and Florida, it would have become a major hurricane. As it was, because it moved so quickly over the water, it didn't have time to develop. I am absolutely certain that the prayers of God's people pushed that storm more quickly across that open water so that it could not become a monster.

I remember watching Irene's progress all day on October 15, 1999. Some friends telephoned me during the day to ask what I thought was going to happen. Several of them had not believed the Hurricane Irene word. My answer was always the same, "We are about to get hit by Irene." I had no doubt we were about to get hit, no matter what the forecasters said, and no matter what their computer models predicted, I knew they were about to be surprised. But I also knew that it would not be as bad as it could have been.

In the end, our area never did come under a hurricane warning. We were under a hurricane watch and a tropical storm warning, but people, businesses, and local governments do not respond to hurricane watches or tropical storm warnings in South Florida. A hurricane warning is needed to activate all of our varied hurricane readiness plans. Without a hurricane warning, business and government hurricane contingency plans were not implemented. Businesses and schools stayed open, and life went on as usual in Broward County.[2]

When the hurricane hit our area by surprise at about 4:00 PM, people were just getting out of work. Some people actually died without ever knowing that they were in a hurricane. Visibility was so bad as workers attempted to drive home from work, that several drove into canals and drowned. You can still read news reports about Hurricane Irene at hurricaneirene.com, the website we maintain for this historical purpose.

At the end of the day, the National Hurricane Center determined that Irene was barely a category one hurricane when it hit our area. The very worst part of the hurricane hit the northeast corner of Broward County, Deerfield Beach, and the southeast corner of Palm Beach County, Boca Raton. Eight people died in the hurricane. The South Florida

---

[2] One letter to the editor in the South Florida Sun-Sentinel captured the chaos of that day: On Friday, the Bette Midler concert was scheduled to be held at the National Car Rental Center. All calls to the center were answered with a recorded message saying, "The Bette Midler concert will be held. Should a hurricane warning be issued, this could change." So. . . like hundreds of others, we drove along Panther Parkway trying to enter the arena parking areas . . . all the entrances were blocked . . . Finally, spying an official vehicle, . . . I was then informed that the concert had "just now" been canceled. *As a result,* the Sawgrass Expressway (as well as Florida's Turnpike and Interstate 95) -- with trees down in one lane and visibility near zero -- was filled with tense people wondering why our lives had been risked in the first place.

counties sustained hundreds of millions of dollars in storm damage. But because of the prayers of God's people, the catastrophic vision that the Lord gave to a twelve-year-old girl never happened. God was there in the midst of the storm.

The following headline and story in the October 17, 1999 edition of the South Florida Sun-Sentinel captured the surprise:

Storm Caught Us, Forecasters Well Off Guard

She surprised us.

Although they knew Irene was in the neighborhood, officials posted no hurricane warnings for South Florida. No one put up shutters. The usual stampede for supplies did not materialize.

Despite satellite imagery, sophisticated radar and surveillance planes, forecasters expected Hurricane Irene to pelt the west coast, not mess up our back yard so badly.

So, how did such a major storm sneak up on us?

Specialists at the National Hurricane Center say because the system lacked strong steering currents and had an undefined center, the blob-like Irene swerved off its forecast track and caught them off guard.

"Early on, none of the computer models that we use for our forecast showed the hurricane approaching South Florida," said Colin McAdie, the center's research meteorologist.

"In addition to that, the system had not been well-defined from the beginning. The center reformed several times when it was still south of Cuba. That made it a difficult forecast," he said.

As late as Friday afternoon, forecasters and residents alike thought the storm would parallel the west coast of Florida and possibly hit the Tampa area.

As a result, there were no long lines at grocery, hardware or home improvement stores Thursday night or Friday morning. Few, if any, people put up shutters or boarded windows.

Despite warnings of heavy rains, people went about their business for the most part. Then the winds kicked up Friday afternoon and the storm's wrath struck in time to clog up rush hour.

Though they were carefully monitoring the storm, emergency managers in Miami-Dade, Broward and Palm Beach counties ordered no evacuations because no hurricane warnings were issued.

Irene was such a surprise, that ten years after the storm, the Sun-Sentinel published this remembrance on October 15, 2009:

Many are sure to remember that Friday.

Hurricane Irene came barging into town with torrential downpours, gusty winds and an element of surprise.

That was on Oct. 15, 1999 - 10 years ago today.

The storm produced 10 to 20 inches of rain and caused severe widespread flooding. More than 700,000 homes and businesses lost power.

And eight people were killed. Five were electrocuted and three drove vehicles into canals. Additionally, tornadoes injured three people in Broward County.

Irene surprised many because they weren't expecting a hurricane, even though they knew a storm was approaching.

At the time, some criticized the National Hurricane Center for that.

But forecasters noted they had issued a tropical storm warning and that most of South Florida experienced just that, a tropical storm, not a hurricane.

While it is natural that the National Hurricane Center would defend itself in such a way, the truth is that without divine intervention, a category four-monster storm would have slammed into South Florida during rush hour traffic. It would have leveled an unprepared community, not only because almost no one had put shutters up, but also because category four storms have a propensity to do just that.

When I sent my final fax and letter to Broward's churches, I ended with this note:

> I wanted to add a message of thanks for your part in the Hurricane Irene drama. We first publicized the dreams outside of our congregation back in early March of this year. I asked people to read the dreams, and to take up the call to prayer if they believed God was speaking. I thank you for not only receiving the dreams, but for praying along with us.
>
> Our first official prayer meeting was March 21. The next was September 12. The last was October 14. Irene hit on October 15. Each of the meetings was powerful and accomplished a part of the purpose that we had set. That purpose was to intercede so that there would be no hurricane, and if there was, that it would not be devastating. I believe that the Lord answered our prayers. God gave us an opportunity to "stand in the gap" for our communities. God is sovereign, but he has chosen to give us authority in prayer. As we prayed we took the opportunity he lovingly gave us.
>
> I am personally saddened by the seven lives (so far reported) that were lost because of this hurricane. We knew that unity and prayer could defeat the plan of the enemy to release a lot of death. We achieved a level of

unity and prayer that severely diminished the tragedy. The toll could have been much higher with even a slightly more powerful storm. But, of course every life is precious, so I am still saddened. If there is a next time for something like this, I will pray even more persistently that lives be spared. I know many of you will do the same. We can celebrate this victory while at the same time mourning with those who mourn. God is love. He has demonstrated it yet again. Thanks for picking up the call to prayer.

New Dawn Community Church, and a broad coalition of churches in Broward County, had accomplished God's purposes. We had bound on earth what he had bound in heaven.

7

AN IRREVOCABLE CALLING

In the aftermath of our call to prayer, things returned to normal. We certainly had a heightened appreciation for God's intervention in the affairs of men. But other than a rather awkward moment of recognition at the same clergy group that I had first briefed about Irene a year earlier, we slipped back into the relative obscurity of normal congregational life. God had used us to accomplish his purposes, and for the moment, we were ready to step away from the spotlight.

However, I was not willing to relinquish the intercessory authority that God had given to us. I believed the Apostle Paul when he told us, **"God's gifts and his call are irrevocable" (Romans 11:29)**. I knew that God didn't give gifts and callings just so that he could take them away again. When he gives you a victory, he gives you something to build on, not something to walk away from. I knew he had given us something that we needed to develop.

I didn't realize it at the time, but there were people who did not like the fact that God had used us in such an obvious way. There were even some in our congregation who did not believe God would use us again. I remember one instance when a man attempted to correct me over my belief. He believed that we could have no assurance that God would use us again. I began to realize that this is a common belief about how God works. It may be common, but it is wrong. Those who truly believe this will always walk with little faith and little power in their lives.

I believe God builds on our experiences. There are two key truths in scripture that have given me this conviction. I have already mentioned the first. I believe what Paul taught: The gifts and call of God are irrevocable. I believe that the Bible makes this clear in many different ways. I especially appreciate how Elijah's life demonstrates this truth.

Elijah's Irrevocable Calling

Elijah was an amazing man living during an incredibly difficult time in Israel's history. He courageously stood up to the evil authorities of his day, and achieved great victories for the Lord. Who can forget Elijah's encounter with the prophets of Baal and Asherah on Mount Carmel (see 1 Kings 18:18-40)? Who can forget how fire fell from heaven and consumed Elijah's sacrifice? His is a story of calling and power.

And yet his story does not end there. As the Apostle James reminded us, Elijah was a man just like us, and subject to the vagaries of our human condition. When Jezebel threatened, he ran. He was so discouraged that he fled to Mount Horeb and turned in his resignation. The Apostle Paul tells us that when Elijah was at Horeb, he **"appealed against Israel" (Romans 11:2).** He turned from prophetic intercessor to prophetic accuser. As a result, God accepted his resignation and instructed Elijah how to prepare Israel for his departure.

If anyone could forfeit his call and gifts, it should have been Elijah. He had been called to stand in the gap for Israel. Like Moses before him, he was supposed to reflect God's heart to Israel. But where Moses had stood in the gap and asked God not to condemn Israel, Elijah complained that he was the only one left. The Apostle Paul understood what Elijah was doing. He was interceding against Israel. He was a witness for the prosecution, calling down the wrath of God on Israel. No wonder the Lord accepted his resignation; Elijah had lost his heart for the job.

As the book of 2 Kings opens, we encounter Elijah once again. Elijah has been working at preparing Israel for his departure, but he still confronted kings. In this instance, the king of Israel, Ahaziah, had injured himself and sought insight about his injury from a pagan god. Elijah intercepted the king's messenger and sent the message that the king would die. When the king realized that the man was Elijah, he sent a captain and his fifty men to arrest Elijah. The captain and his fifty men confronted Elijah. Let's pick up the story here:

> **The captain went up to Elijah, who was sitting on the top of a hill, and said to him, "Man of God, the king says, 'Come down!'"**
>
> **Elijah answered the captain, "If I am a man of God, may fire come down from heaven and consume you and your fifty men!" Then fire fell from heaven and consumed the captain and his men.**

At this the king sent to Elijah another captain with his fifty men. The captain said to him, "Man of God, this is what the king says, 'Come down at once!'"

"If I am a man of God," Elijah replied, "may fire come down from heaven and consume you and your fifty men!" Then the fire of God fell from heaven and consumed him and his fifty men.

So the king sent a third captain with his fifty men. This third captain went up and fell on his knees before Elijah. "Man of God," he begged, "please have respect for my life and the lives of these fifty men, your servants! See, fire has fallen from heaven and consumed the first two captains and all their men. But now have respect for my life!"

The angel of the LORD said to Elijah, "Go down with him; do not be afraid of him." So Elijah got up and went down with him to the king. (2 Kings 1:10-15)

I don't believe you can find a clearer example of the fact that the gifts and callings of God are irrevocable than in this story of Elijah. When he had called fire down on Mount Carmel, he had gained authority before God. That authority became so much a part of Elijah's gifts and callings, that he could use that gift at need.

Here is what I see in this story: When the Lord gives authority to us, he releases that authority to us. It becomes ours. Elijah's use of heavenly fire demonstrates this point. In the same way, I know that God has given us authority over the storm, and that authority is now irrevocably ours.

The Various Sizes of Faith

The second key truth that bolstered my conviction that God had granted us continuing authority over storms, is found in the very definitions of faith and how faith works practically in our lives. Jesus clearly taught that there are various sizes of faith. By its very nature, faith must continue in any manifestation of the supernatural that it experiences. To do less constitutes little faith.

Little Faith

Jesus revealed a great deal about faith when he chided those who had little of it. On six different occasions Jesus told people they had little faith. In every instance he was speaking to a people who had a special covenant with God: Israel. These people had history with God, and yet still had little faith. When we look more closely at several of these instances, we learn just what constitutes little faith.

In the Sermon on the Mount, Jesus revealed how inappropriate it is for God's people to worry about food or clothing. After pointing to the beauty of the flowers around them, Jesus asked, **"If that is how God clothes the grass of the field, which is here today and tomorrow is thrown into the fire, will he not much more clothe you, O you of little faith?" (Matthew 6:30).**

His point is clear. Every one of the people around Jesus had observed God's care of birds and flowers. Their experience taught them that God takes good care of such relatively minor things. Thus, it is not rational to conclude that he would treat his chosen people with less care. When the people of Jesus' day worried about food and clothing, they did not live up to their experience of God's care, and they were not being rational. Jesus summed it up by saying they had little faith.

When Jesus calmed the storm we see these same themes. A severe storm on the sea of Galilee was testing the mettle of Jesus' disciples. As the storm began to overwhelm them, the disciples cried out to the sleeping Jesus to save them. As Jesus woke up he said to them, **"You of little faith, why are you so afraid?" (Matthew 8:26).** Then, with a word, he calmed the storm.

From a non-faith perspective, it is quite apparent why the disciples were afraid. Huge waves were swamping their boat. The experienced fishermen among them understood the gravity of the situation. Over the years, they had seen friends and neighbors in their fishing community disappear in tempests such as this one. Because of their experience on the water, they were convinced they were all about to drown. From a purely natural perspective, they were behaving rationally. But the disciples had been living the supernatural with Jesus for quite some time. They had history with Jesus— lots of it. Yet they allowed their previous life experience to trump that supernatural experience with Jesus. Because they had experienced his great love and his great power, it was irrational for them to believe that he would allow them to drown. They were not living up to their supernatural experience with Jesus. They had little faith.

This problem plagued the disciples. The most obvious example of this is recorded in Matthew 16. Jesus had just finished feeding five thousand men, in addition to the women and children, with five loaves of bread and a few fish. He had followed that miracle up with the feeding of the four thousand under similar conditions. Yet when the disciples forgot to bring bread for a journey, they concluded that this would leave them bereft of lunch. Jesus quite explicitly leads them down the road of logic to show them the type of faith they were demonstrating.

> . . . Jesus asked, "You of little faith, why are you talking among yourselves about having no bread? Do you still not understand? Don't you remember the five loaves for the five thousand, and how many basketfuls you gathered? Or the seven loaves for the four thousand, and how many basketfuls you gathered? (Matthew 16:8-10)

Jesus could have added the miraculous catch of fish, and the many other supernatural wonders that had been demonstrated to these disciples, but he focused only on the most applicable miracles. Jesus had fed tens of thousands of people with less than a grocery bag of food. It is only logical to conclude, that in a pinch, he could handle lunch for a dozen. More than that, their experience of his generous care of all these people made it impossible to assume that he would callously ignore the plight of his closest disciples. The littleness of their faith was staggering. But often, so is ours.

Jesus once said, **"When the Son of Man comes, will he find faith on the earth?" (Luke 18:8)**. While faith may be at a premium when he returns, I don't believe he will have any problem finding *little faith*. We can easily find that all around us. It occurs whenever we, like Jesus' disciples, do not live up to our experience of God's love and his power. I have seen many examples of indisputable miraculous healing. I have seen my own family touched in amazing ways, and I have felt his healing hand personally. Yet there are times when I am assaulted with concerns about my own or my family's health that I am tempted to step into worry. Since I have experienced God's love and his power in this area, if I do step into worry, I am demonstrating little faith. It is rational to believe that God is faithful and consistent in these areas. It is irrational to believe that God is capricious or fickle. For this reason, we can build our faith for the future upon our experiences of his love and power in the past. If we do not do this, we are demonstrating little faith.

This applies to every area of our life. If the Lord has provided a miraculous financial deliverance for us, we can rationally expect that he will be faithful in this area again. That is faith. If the Lord has provided physical healing, we can rationally expect the Healer to be faithful in this area again. That is faith. When we experience the Lord's faithfulness in an area, it is only faith to expect that the Lord will repeat that kindness.

This truth is exactly the reason that Jesus told Peter he had little faith right after he walked on water. From our perspective, Peter demonstrated incredible faith when he stepped out of the boat onto a stormy sea. Yet, when Jesus stooped down to pull the sinking Peter back to the surface of the waves, he said to him, **"You of little faith" (Matthew 14:31).** There is little doubt that when Peter stepped out of the boat he was demonstrating faith, perhaps even great faith. His quick demotion to little faith was found in his irrational doubt. In the midst of miraculously breaking several laws of physics, he began to believe those laws were more powerful than this miracle. He didn't live up to the level of his miraculous experience, even while he was experiencing it. That is little faith.

Great Faith

If little faith is irrationally living below your experience of God, then, conversely, great faith is rationally living above your level of experience. Jesus clearly demonstrates this when he responded to two gentiles who walked in great faith.

It is not coincidence that Jesus only applies the great faith label to gentiles. The gentiles of Jesus' day had little experience of the true God. The Roman centurion (see Matthew 8:5-10) and the Syrophoenician woman (see Matthew 15:21-28) grew up in nations with demonic understandings of deity. Their national gods were demanding, erratic, and vicious. These pagan cultures bribed and placated their gods, rather than loving or trusting them. Their understanding of God's goodness and grace was limited. Yet both these individuals stepped beyond their experience. Still, they did not do this irrationally; they gave solid reasons for their steps of faith,

When Jesus encountered the centurion, his servant was sick. Jesus acted according to Jewish custom and agreed to go to the servant's side. In Jewish culture, it was normal for those who prayed for healing to make a personal appearance (see Matthew 9:18). Jesus usually followed this custom in order to remove unnecessary barriers to faith. He did what he could to encourage the faith of true seekers.

When the centurion, who had not grown up in covenant relationship with God, sought Jesus' help, he was demonstrating faith. Jesus responded to this faith in his normal fashion. However, the centurion soon demonstrated greatness in his faith.

> **The centurion replied, "Lord, I do not deserve to have you come under my roof. But just say the word, and my servant will be healed." (Matthew 8:8)**

With these words the centurion demonstrated great faith. With his first request, the centurion demonstrated that he had moved beyond his own cultural experience and now believed in the goodness of God. With his second request, he demonstrated that he had moved beyond even the Jewish cultural understanding of how God worked. Whereas Jewish theology expected some form of contact to initiate a miracle, this centurion believed a word spoken at a distance would do.

To those who traveled with Jesus, this may have seemed like presumption. How dare this centurion presume to tell Jesus how to operate his ministry? But this wasn't presumption. Presumption is irrational in its character. Presumption moves beyond our experience of God in irrational ways. The centurion did not do this. Instead, he offered a rational explanation for his belief.

> **For I myself am a man under authority, with soldiers under me. I tell this one, 'Go,' and he goes; and that one, 'Come,' and he comes. I say to my servant, 'Do this,' and he does it." (Matthew 8:9)**

The centurion recognized the nature of authority. If the centurion, with only a word, could affect outcomes at a distance, then Jesus should be able to do the same thing. The centurion stepped ahead of his experience of God as he applied his understanding of authority to God's Kingdom in a logical way. That is great faith.

The Syrophoenician woman demonstrated this same logical application of truth. When Jesus had insulted her by comparing her to a dog, she said,

> **"Yes, Lord," she said, "but even the dogs eat the crumbs that fall from their masters' table." (Matthew 15:27)**

When Jesus purposely baited her, she refused to choke on the bait. Instead she demonstrated faith. She recognized that it would only take supernatural crumbs for an almighty God to heal her daughter. Then she demonstrated great faith. She inferred some things about God's Kingdom based upon Jesus' own words. If a dog's master allows him to eat the crumbs that fall below the table, how much more would a righteous and merciful God provide the crumbs of his supernatural grace to people in need? Rather than turning away insulted and sad, she lived beyond her experience of

God and received her answer. She also demonstrated great faith.

In essence, great faith stands on the foundation of our experience of God, builds a reasonable case for things we have not yet experienced, and takes action based upon that belief. But while Jesus applauded great faith and was pleased by it, he does not demand great faith from us. It only takes faith to please God.

Faith

John the apostle penned the words that speak of our experience of God. He wrote, **"We love because he first loved us" (see 1 John 4:19).** Faith responds to the grace that God has given. It experiences something of God, and then responds to it. We became Christians through this process. We experienced the promise of God's forgiveness and love, and faith lived up to this experience by receiving Jesus into our hearts. We now live by faith because Christianity is experiential in nature. He continually invades our world with his love; in faith we respond to that love. If we respond commensurate to our level of experience, we have faith. If we respond above our level of experience, we have great faith. If we respond below our level of experience, we have little faith.

The writer to the Hebrews tells us, **"Without faith it is impossible to please God (Hebrews 11:6).** This is more than an axiom to inspire a more committed faith life; it is the foundation of our Christian walk. Christians live by faith from start to finish (see Romans 1:17). Jude wrote, **"But you, dear friends, build yourselves up in your most holy faith" (Jude 1:20).** I believe that when we better understand the process of faith, we can better build our faith. It is apparent that greatness or littleness of faith is not found in the size of the supernatural events in which we are involved, but rather in how well we are living up to our experience of God and his faithfulness.

The people of New Dawn Community Church had an experience with God. They had seen him protect them through a storm. They had received his authority to deal with the storm. When we believe that God will continue to deal with us in this fashion, it is only faith. It believes that the gifts and callings of God are irrevocable.

8

CONCLUSIONS

I am writing these words as we approach the fifteenth anniversary of Hurricane Irene's visit to our area. Our history since 1999 has been filled with wonderful victories and not-so-fun learning experiences. We have grown even more firmly in our conviction that the Lord has given us a job to do, and we are doing it to the best of our ability.

This short book covers, in very brief form, the first four years in the development of New Dawn Community Church. I could write about many more storms and other supernatural events, and more than likely I will in the future. However, this particular book is written for a particular purpose. It reveals a calling, and it invites you to join with us in that calling.

At the time that I am writing this chapter in 2014, weather forecasters are openly speculating that we have entered into a shift in the hurricane pattern for the Atlantic basin. This year has been spectacularly slow, as far as hurricane seasons go. Last year was even slower. Forecasters do not understand the shift. I do understand the shift. God's people are learning to use their authority.

An Incontrovertible Fact

I also wrote this book for another reason. The cover of this book makes the claim that the Irene story is incontrovertible proof that God still speaks today. This is true for several reasons.

First, the events as described unquestionably happened. There are dozens of pastors and hundreds of churches with thousands of members who knew about the prediction before Irene hit. They are witnesses to the predictions about Irene and the facts as they have been presented in this book. In addition, the fact that a local NBC news affiliate picked up the story, and ran their interview—an interview that can still be viewed today—almost two weeks before Irene even formed, is also evidence of the veracity of this report. It is not possible to deny these events. This is history. It truly happened.

The second reason that I believe that the evidence that God still speaks to his people is incontrovertible, concerns the prediction itself. It could not have happened by chance. The odds against anyone randomly predicting the things we predicted about Irene are astronomically high. It would be impossible for someone to pick out a hurricane name at random a year in advance, and correctly predict the things we did about Irene. Consider what we knew. We knew that the ninth storm of 1999, a storm that would be named Irene, would not only form, but that it would become a hurricane. We not only knew that it would make landfall, we knew where it would hit, even though such a prediction about a storm that hasn't formed is impossible. And to make it even more impossible, we knew it would hit without the National Hurricane Center issuing a hurricane warning for our area.

When you add that fact to all the others, there is no doubt that we had supernatural information. It is categorically impossible that we could have guessed all these details correctly about a particular named storm.

I'm emphasizing this for a reason. People, even Christians, can be very uncomfortable with the idea that God still speaks to his people, but my congregation and thousands of other people are witnesses to the fact that he does, and now through this book and the evidence it presents, so are you. The evidence as presented more than supports the fact that God still speaks to his people.

Why would God speak to us about such a storm? The answer is that he loves us. John 3:16 is far more than a platitude when it says, **"God so loved the world that he gave his one and only Son, that whoever believes in him shall not perish but have eternal life."** This is an incredible truth, and it is an incredible invitation.

The incredible truth is that God sent his Son, Jesus, into this world to become one of us. It is no secret that the world has a sin problem. You only need to read current headlines to understand that. Even more importantly, you only need to look into the mirror to understand that. We, each of us, are prone to selfish action and outright rebellion against God's plans and purposes for our life. This fact separates us from God. But in his love our Father provided a Savior. Jesus came into the world and fulfilled all the requirements of God's law perfectly, then he died to pay for our debt. He then rose again to seal his victory. He came as a man so that he might represent us. He came as God so that his payment for our debt might count for us all.

The incredible invitation is found in the fact that the Father now invites us to believe that Jesus is our Savior. When we receive his payment for our sins, when we receive him, our debt is swept away, the Holy Spirit takes up residence in our spirit, and he begins to change us in ways that we never thought possible. I would encourage you to agree with Jesus that you need him, and ask him into your heart on this day.

God's love motivated him to provide Jesus as our Savior, and it also moved him to speak to us about Hurricane Irene. Paul explains this truth in Romans 8 when he reminds us that God's love extends beyond the cross into every aspect of our lives. Paul wrote, **"He who did not spare his own Son, but gave him up for us all—how will he not also, along with him, graciously give us all things?" (Romans 8:32).** Paul reveals an astonishing truth to us. The Father not only provided for our salvation, he also provided for our life. He is a good Father. As such, he will always provide aid and direction to those who seek it. He will also, always, look for those who will stand in the gap for others.

Following Through

You may not yet know the fullness of your calling, but you can begin to pray for your area of influence. You may not know all of your spiritual gifts, but you can use your God-given authority to protect your geographic area. You can grow in the authority that God has given to his Church by exercising that authority. He has given us the keys. We can either use them or ignore them. When we ignore them, bad things happen. When we use them, bad things do not happen and the Father receives incredible glory.

This book contains a challenge. After you read it, you can return to business as usual, or you can pick up the keys of spiritual authority that God has given to you, and use them.

The Lord's plan is simple. He has given the keys of authority to his Church. He expects us to use them. We are his feet on the earth. Let's walk as he intends.

APPENDIX ONE

THE MARCH 1, 1999 FACSIMILE

New Dawn

Community Church

11030 Wiles Road, Coral Springs, Florida 33076 • (954) 753-7729

Randal Cutter, *Pastor*

March 1, 1999

To: Area Church and Ministry Leaders
Re: Hurricane Irene Forecast
From: Randal Cutter
Message:

The following pages contain four dreams which various individuals had which seem to point to the fact that we could be in for a visit from a Hurricane named Irene in 1999.

Please review the following dreams. I believe that God has not stopped communicating through dreams to his people. I realize that this belief is open to theological dispute. However, please review the following even if you don't believe that God communicates through dreams. Then you can throw it away if you don't agree that God is saying something to us.

If you believe God is sending us a warning to pray against a hurricane Irene, and you want to join us in the effort, please call or fax us. We are having a joint meeting with Good News Church on March 21 (South East Corner of Broward Blvd. and Hwy 441 - just behind the shopping center) at 7:00 pm to discuss what we believe God is saying, and to pray. If you are interested, stop by.

Phone (954) 753-7729
Fax (954) 345-2562
E-mail: NewDawnCh@aol.com

http://www.ncwdawn.org

Number of Pages: 4 pages including this cover sheet

DREAM ONE (Randal Cutter, Pastor of New Dawn Community Church)

During the early morning hours of August 11, 1998, I had a vivid dream that Dawn and I were standing in front of our home. The sky was filled with gray storm clouds from an approaching hurricane. I was deciding whether to shut the hurricane shutters on our home. I had a very strong conviction in the dream that this hurricane wasn't really going to hit. No matter what the forecaster's were saying, I was convinced we were wasting our time. The dream ended as I decided to shut the hurricane shutters out of prudence, rather than from any conviction that there was danger. Even as I was doing this I had a strong impression that there truly was a hurricane coming to the Fort Lauderdale area which would hit.

I woke from that dream convinced that the dream had not been symbolic, but had truly been about actual hurricanes. I believe the Lord was telling me that I should be aware of two hurricanes. One of those hurricanes would be a hurricane which the forecasters said was going to hit. But it would not. The second hurricane would be one that truly would hit our area.

DREAM TWO (Dawn Cutter)

On August 20, as Tropical Storm Bonnie was heading toward hurricane status and just beginning to be a concern to South Florida, Dawn dreamed about her sisters, Bonnie and Irene. This is the dream as she wrote it:

I had a dream that Irene came to visit unexpectedly. I was surprised that Irene came and that Bonnie didn't. She brought a deer steak, but it was not enough for everyone. I went to the freezer to add to that which Irene had brought.

Important information: In this dream, Dawn's sister Irene, who lives in Wisconsin, paid us an unexpected visit. Dawn was surprised because she knows that her other sister, Bonnie, would love to visit us. Irene would not normally come to visit. She doesn't travel that much and has expressed no interest in coming to Florida. Bonnie is the oldest. Irene is second oldest. As we know, Bonnie (the hurricane) did not come to South Florida.

More important information: The hurricane for 1999 which starts with the letter "I", should we get that far in the alphabet, is Irene. One other bit of information we figured out months after these dreams: August 11, the date of the first dream which I had, is the birthday of Dawn's sister Irene. This seems to tie the two dreams tightly together and highlights Irene.

IMPRESSIONS (Randal Cutter)

Based upon these two dreams I had a strong conviction that Hurricane Georges was not coming to Fort Lauderdale when it appeared on the horizon. Irene was the one I was watching. I told my elders before our meetings one Sunday that Georges was not going to hit us. I also intended on telling the congregation on that day, but I didn't write it down -- so naturally, I forgot. This was on the Sunday before Georges threatened South Florida. Georges wasn't even a minor threat at that time. Even when it became a threat I was convinced that it was not going to hit. Even when the hurricane warnings went up I could not shake the conviction. I was in North Carolina at a retreat center at the time. If I had thought it was going to hit, I would have gone home. I wouldn't normally leave my family to fend for themselves in a hurricane.

I kept telling Dawn that I believed it wasn't going to hit. She believed it wasn't going to hit either. I told her to have the office staff release that word from the office to anyone that they had contact with. I didn't want our folks to get any panic on them. I also told Dawn to shut the hurricane shutters on our house, though I thought it was a waste of time. I didn't want a miss read on my part to endanger my family.

Of course, Georges missed, at the last second, in a way that made Southeast Florida forecasters say, "Mea Culpa." I became even more convinced that God was speaking about hurricanes in our dreams since this seemed to be a partial fulfillment of dream #1. I began to ask God for more confirmations on Irene.

DREAM THREE (Joyce Moyer)

We received this dream during October from a colleague in Wisconsin. We had been asking God for more confirmations. My friend did not know this. His wife, Joyce, had a dream about a hurricane. This is what his e-mail said:

Joyce had a dream last night (eve. of 10-19) that a storm (hurricane) was coming. Somehow she was told (It was just told to her); "there's a hurricane coming that is going to do what the last one didn't do, (the one that passed)." After Joyce heard this, I was talking to you on the phone, suggesting that you come to our place to visit for a while. Joyce was impressed by the fact that this one would level wherever it hit. Your response was that you and the family were just going to stand in the shower. [End of dream]
We will pray for you guys, and I strongly suggest we get the word out for prayer. Joyce has received so many literal warnings and information like this released in her dreams that it's almost scary. [End of e-mail]

Important information: Based upon Romans 5, I often refer to the fact that we stand in a shower of God's grace. That is what immediately came to mind when I read the note.

DREAM FOUR (Teenaged Girl)

A twelve-year old member of our congregation had this dream on October 2. I did not get the dream until after I read my friend's e-mail. That is why I call it dream four, even though it was chronologically earlier than Joyce's dream.

In the dream this young lady and her friend were walking along the road in Deerfield Beach, just to the north of Fort Lauderdale, and just north and east of the city of Coral Springs. As they walked they were surveying the damage which had been done by a hurricane. They saw houses which were torn apart. As they passed by a hotel they saw floors, beds other things from the hotel in the street and on the beach. They saw a great deal of damage. Then they returned to her friend's home. Her friend's father was watching reports of the damage on a portable television set. The newscaster was mentioning that the hurricane had been a surprise. It had hit Broward County and south Palm Beach county. The newscaster also mentioned that it was a category four hurricane with wind speeds of 180 to 200 miles per hour. [end of dream]

Important information: According to the Saffir-Simpson scale, a category four hurricane has sustained wind speeds between 131 and 155 miles per hour. A category five hurricane has sustained winds above 155 miles per hour. In a strong category four hurricane, wind gusts of up to 200 miles per hour could certainly be expected, but that is not what is explicitly stated in the dream as it was written.

According to the Saffir-Simpson scale, a category four hurricane has (Sustained winds of 131 to 155 miles per hour) a potential storm surge between 13 and 18 feet above normal. The damage from such a storm would be extreme. Homes would be heavily damaged. Mobile homes would be completely destroyed. Some shrubs, large trees, and all signs would be blown down. Terrain lower than ten feet above sea level may be flooded as far as six miles inland. This description sounds bad until you consider the category five alternative. According to the same scale, a category five hurricane has sustained winds greater than 155 miles per hour. The storm surge would potentially be more than 18 feet above normal. The damage would be catastrophic with complete roof failure on many residences and industrial buildings. Some complete building failures would occur, with small utility buildings blown away or overturned. All shrubs, trees, and signs would be blown down. There would be flood danger for all dwellings on low ground up to ten miles inland. It goes without saying that the expected death toll in such a storm would be high.

Other important information: In the dream which Dawn had (Dream #2), Irene brought along some deer steaks. In this dream, the young lady is walking along Deer-field Beach. God has quite the sense of humor.

CONCLUSION

We have had other dreams which seem to confirm that a hurricane is an imminent danger for our area. These are the first ones which God gave to us which put us on the scent. We believe he is speaking.

Why would God speak to us in this way? The answer is found in the book of Jonah. God spoke through a reluctant prophet in order to get a city to repent and turn to God - and thus the city avoided destruction. I do not claim to be a prophet. I am a pastor who has been allowed to have one dream, and coordinate several more. I believe God's purposes for Nineveh are the same for us. He wants us to examine our ways, humble ourselves, and take responsibility for our land. I believe he wants us to pray that this hurricane never materialize.

The best possible end to all of this is that we humble ourselves and pray, and that a hurricane named Irene never materializes on our horizon. It would then be nice if we could praise God for answered prayer. If a hurricane named Irene never comes, some might say,, "Oh, those dreams really amounted to nothing." I can live with that . . . . I certainly don't like the alternative. Let's pray together.

To God be the Glory.

Randal Cutter, Pastor
New Dawn Community Church   e-mail: NewDawnCh @aol.com
11030 Wiles Road
Coral Springs, FL 33076   http://www.newdawn.org
(954) 753-7729 Phone
(954) 345-2562 Fax

APPENDIX TWO

HURRICANE IRENE'S TRACK

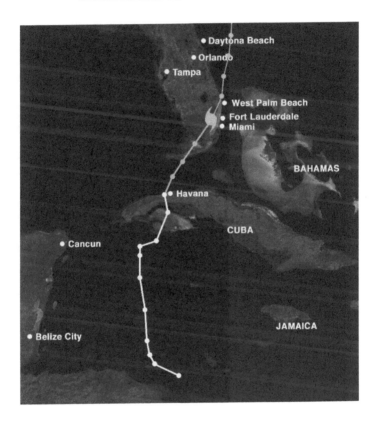

APPENDIX THREE

HURRICANE IRENE WATCHES AND WARNINGS

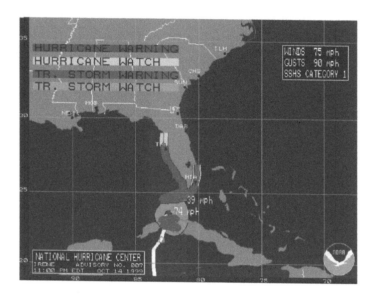

ABOUT THE AUTHOR

Randal Cutter is the founding pastor of New Dawn Community Church.

Randal is a dynamic teacher of God's truth. He has studied Greek and Hebrew extensively, and informs his teaching with appropriate references. He has a theologian's perspective on biblical truth, and a pastor's heart for applying living truth.

In addition to his pastoral duties at New Dawn, he is also an Elder for the MorningStar Fellowship of Ministries, an organization that provides relational covering for ministries around the world. The MorningStar Fellowship of Ministries was founded by Rick Joyner in 1995. Randal has been an ordained member of the Fellowship of Ministries since its inception in 1995. He is also an adjunct professor of the Greek language for MorningStar University's College of Theology. He has travelled extensively to teach the Word, and impart clarity, prophetic vision, and insight.

Randal has been married to Dawn since 1980. They have three children, Alyssa, Linea, and Joshua.

You may contact Randal at:
New Dawn Community Church
9335 W. Sample Road
Coral Springs, FL 33065
(954) 753-7729
NewDawn@NewDawn.org

You may see his current teaching messages at: NewDawn.org
Follow his blog at: RandalCutter.com